I0470240

Name:

_____

Success is no accident... The
price of success is hard work
and dedication. And you can
achieve both.

Inside You'll Find

Inside You'll Find (cont.)

"If you are going to be successful in big things, you first need to develop the habit in small things..."

- Just Creative Journals

Build A New Habit

Habit:_____

Take some time to write down a good habit that you want to build or a bad habit that you want to break. Each day that you've achieved this habit-goal, color in or tick one of the stars below. This visual representation of our progress will make it easier for us to build a good habit or break a bad one!

Build A New Habit

Habit: _____

Take some time to write down a good habit that you want to build or a bad habit that you want to break. Each day that you've achieved this habit-goal, color in or tick one of the stars below. This visual representation of our progress will make it easier for us to build a good habit or break a bad one!

Build A New Habit

Habit: _____

Take some time to write down a good habit that you want to build or a bad habit that you want to break. Each day that you've achieved this habit-goal, color in or tick one of the stars below. This visual representation of our progress will make it easier for us to build a good habit or break a bad one!

Build A New Habit

Habit:_____

Take some time to write down a good habit that you want to build or a bad habit that you want to break. Each day that you've achieved this habit-goal, color in or tick one of the stars below. This visual representation of our progress will make it easier for us to build a good habit or break a bad one!

Build A New Habit

Habit:_____

Take some time to write down a good habit that you want to build or a bad habit that you want to break. Each day that you've achieved this habit-goal, color in or tick one of the stars below. This visual representation of our progress will make it easier for us to build a good habit or break a bad one!

Build A New Habit

Habit:_____

Take some time to write down a good habit that you want to build or a bad habit that you want to break. Each day that you've achieved this habit-goal, color in or tick one of the stars below. This visual representation of our progress will make it easier for us to build a good habit or break a bad one!

Build A New Habit

Habit:_____

Take some time to write down a good habit that you want to build or a bad habit that you want to break. Each day that you've achieved this habit-goal, color in or tick one of the stars below. This visual representation of our progress will make it easier for us to build a good habit or break a bad one!

Build A New Habit

Habit: _____

Take some time to write down a good habit that you want to build or a bad habit that you want to break. Each day that you've achieved this habit-goal, color in or tick one of the stars below. This visual representation of our progress will make it easier for us to build a good habit or break a bad one!

Build A New Habit

Habit:_____

Take some time to write down a good habit that you want to build or a bad habit that you want to break. Each day that you've achieved this habit-goal, color in or tick one of the stars below. This visual representation of our progress will make it easier for us to build a good habit or break a bad one!

Build A New Habit

Habit: _____

Take some time to write down a good habit that you want to build or a bad habit that you want to break. Each day that you've achieved this habit-goal, color in or tick one of the stars below. This visual representation of our progress will make it easier for us to build a good habit or break a bad one!

Your Vision Statement

Do you feel like you are walking through life in the dark? Or that you have no clear vision and going around in circles? Do you feel lost? Then you need to work on your vision-statement. A vision statement is a declaration of our objectives and to guide our internal decision-making, whether it is in our business or personal life. Our vision statement should provide a clear idea of our path forward. Our vision statement should also be a constant reminder that the end goal is bigger than the everyday challenges. Every day is an adventure, but sometimes that adventure leads us to a dead end. On those days we need to remember the passion we have – whether it is to launch our own business or whether we already have our own business or whatever personal goals we have – the values that helped get us to where we are and the vision we have for a better future.

Make Some Notes On Your Vision Statement

_____

_____

_____

_____

_____

_____

_____

Your Vision Statement (cont.)

_____

_____

_____

_____

_____

_____

_____

_____

_____

_____

_____

_____

_____

_____

_____

_____

_____

_____

_____

What Is Success?

To some success is having financial freedom, being your own boss and traveling the world. Or having a sustainable income and being able to pay our bills on time. To others, success is staying at home and raising a family.

We need to find *our own meaning* of what success means to us! Many of us base our goals on the success of others and this leads to unhappiness and leading an unfulfilled life.

Here are some questions to help uncover our own beliefs, values and create our own definition of what success means to us. Just let your imagination go…

What Does Success Mean to You?

_____

_____

_____

_____

_____

_____

_____

_____

_____

How Did You Get To Your Definition Of What Success Means To You?

_____

_____

_____

_____

_____

_____

_____

_____

Do You Think You Are Successful? Why?

_____

_____

_____

_____

_____

_____

_____

_____

"Stop looking around you to define what success means to you - the answer lies within..."

- Just Creative Journals

Celebrate Your Talents

We all have unique and different talents. We just need to allow these talents to be celebrated. Stop focusing on what we don't have and celebrate the talents that we do have! Focusing on our strengths will create a shift in our minds, which will lead to more success, confidence and a more fulfilled life.

Let's identify our strengths and help us to get the ball rolling in order to be an even better version of ourselves!

Write Down Some Of Your Best Qualities

_____

_____

_____

_____

_____

_____

_____

_____

_____

_____

_____

What Do You Love Most About Yourself?

_____

_____

_____

_____

_____

_____

_____

_____

_____

What's Great About Your Personal And Business Life?

_____

_____

_____

_____

_____

_____

_____

What Would People Close To You Say About You?

_____
_____
_____
_____
_____
_____
_____
_____
_____

What Is One Of Your Greatest Achievements?

_____
_____
_____
_____
_____
_____
_____
_____
_____

What Are Your Priorities?

_____

_____

_____

_____

_____

_____

_____

_____

_____

What Motivates You?

_____

_____

_____

_____

_____

_____

_____

_____

Setting Goals

Goal: _____

Take some time to write down some of your top goals.
Now think about what action steps you need to take, in
order to achieve your goals?

_____

_____

_____

_____

_____

_____

_____

_____

_____

_____

_____

_____

_____

_____

_____

_____

_____

Setting Goals

Goal: _____

Take some time to write down some of your top goals.
Now think about what action steps you need to take, in
order to achieve your goals?

_____

_____

_____

_____

_____

_____

_____

_____

_____

_____

_____

_____

_____

_____

_____

_____

_____

Setting Goals

Goal: _____

Take some time to write down some of your top goals.
Now think about what action steps you need to take, in
order to achieve your goals?

_____

_____

_____

_____

_____

_____

_____

_____

_____

_____

_____

_____

_____

_____

_____

_____

_____

_____

Setting Goals

Goal: _____

Take some time to write down some of your top goals. Now think about what action steps you need to take, in order to achieve your goals?

_____

_____

_____

_____

_____

_____

_____

_____

_____

_____

_____

_____

_____

_____

_____

_____

_____

_____

Setting Goals

Goal: _____

Take some time to write down some of your top goals.
Now think about what action steps you need to take, in
order to achieve your goals?

_____

_____

_____

_____

_____

_____

_____

_____

_____

_____

_____

_____

_____

_____

_____

_____

_____

_____

Setting Goals

Goal: _____

Take some time to write down some of your top goals.
Now think about what action steps you need to take, in
order to achieve your goals?

_____

_____

_____

_____

_____

_____

_____

_____

_____

_____

_____

_____

_____

_____

_____

_____

_____

_____

Setting Goals

Goal: _____

Take some time to write down some of your top goals. Now think about what action steps you need to take, in order to achieve your goals?

_____

_____

_____

_____

_____

_____

_____

_____

_____

_____

_____

_____

_____

_____

_____

_____

_____

_____

_____

_____

Setting Goals

Goal: _____

Take some time to write down some of your top goals.
Now think about what action steps you need to take, in
order to achieve your goals?

_____

_____

_____

_____

_____

_____

_____

_____

_____

_____

_____

_____

_____

_____

_____

_____

_____

Setting Goals

Goal: _____

Take some time to write down some of your top goals.
Now think about what action steps you need to take, in
order to achieve your goals?

_____

_____

_____

_____

_____

_____

_____

_____

_____

_____

_____

_____

_____

_____

_____

_____

Setting Goals

Goal: _____

Take some time to write down some of your top goals. Now think about what action steps you need to take, in order to achieve your goals?

_____

_____

_____

_____

_____

_____

_____

_____

_____

_____

_____

_____

_____

_____

_____

_____

_____

_____

Identify Your Blockers

We all have those things in life that holds us back. That something that we fear, because we have a fear of failing. That thing that keeps us from taking a leap of faith or making some big life changing decisions…

What Holds You Back?

_____

_____

_____

_____

_____

_____

_____

_____

_____

_____

_____

_____

_____

_____

_____

_____

What Is Something You Really Want to Accomplish, but Are to Afraid to Do?

_____

_____

_____

_____

_____

_____

_____

_____

What Have You Sacrificed in Your Life? Why?

_____

_____

_____

_____

_____

_____

_____

_____

"Don't focus on the chasm before you, focus on the mountain top and spread your wings and fly... Believe in Yourself!"

- Just Creative Journals

Accountability

If we have someone who supports us in our goals, we have a better chance to stay on track, so that we can achieve our goals.

Who Can You Chat To About Your Goals? How Often Will You Share Your Goals And Achievements With Them?

_____

_____

_____

_____

_____

_____

_____

_____

_____

_____

_____

_____

_____

Notes

Believe in Yourself

Write down your thoughts and inspirations here….

_____

_____

_____

_____

_____

_____

_____

_____

_____

_____

_____

_____

_____

_____

_____

_____

_____

_____

Notes

Imagine Yourself Already Having What You Desire

Write down your thoughts and inspirations here….

_____

_____

_____

_____

_____

_____

_____

_____

_____

_____

_____

_____

_____

_____

_____

_____

_____

Notes

Believe in Yourself

Write down your thoughts and inspirations here….

_____

_____

_____

_____

_____

_____

_____

_____

_____

_____

_____

_____

_____

_____

_____

_____

_____

_____

Notes

Imagine Yourself Already Having What You Desire

Write down your thoughts and inspirations here….

_____

_____

_____

_____

_____

_____

_____

_____

_____

_____

_____

_____

_____

_____

_____

_____

_____

_____

Notes

Believe in Yourself

Write down your thoughts and inspirations here....

_____

_____

_____

_____

_____

_____

_____

_____

_____

_____

_____

_____

_____

_____

_____

_____

_____

Notes

Imagine Yourself Already Having What You Desire

Write down your thoughts and inspirations here....

_____

_____

_____

_____

_____

_____

_____

_____

_____

_____

_____

_____

_____

_____

_____

_____

_____

Notes

Believe in Yourself

Write down your thoughts and inspirations here….

_____

_____

_____

_____

_____

_____

_____

_____

_____

_____

_____

_____

_____

_____

_____

_____

_____

_____

_____

_____

Notes

Imagine Yourself Already Having What You Desire

Write down your thoughts and inspirations here….

_____

_____

_____

_____

_____

_____

_____

_____

_____

_____

_____

_____

_____

_____

_____

_____

_____

_____

Notes

Believe in Yourself

Write down your thoughts and inspirations here….

_____

_____

_____

_____

_____

_____

_____

_____

_____

_____

_____

_____

_____

_____

_____

_____

_____

Notes

Imagine Yourself Already Having What You Desire

Write down your thoughts and inspirations here....

_____

_____

_____

_____

_____

_____

_____

_____

_____

_____

_____

_____

_____

_____

_____

_____

_____

_____

Notes

Believe in Yourself

Write down your thoughts and inspirations here....

_____

_____

_____

_____

_____

_____

_____

_____

_____

_____

_____

_____

_____

_____

_____

_____

_____

_____

_____

Notes

Imagine Yourself Already Having What You Desire

Write down your thoughts and inspirations here....

_____

_____

_____

_____

_____

_____

_____

_____

_____

_____

_____

_____

_____

_____

_____

_____

_____

_____

Notes

Believe in Yourself

Write down your thoughts and inspirations here….

_____

_____

_____

_____

_____

_____

_____

_____

_____

_____

_____

_____

_____

_____

_____

_____

_____

Notes

Imagine Yourself Already Having What You Desire

Write down your thoughts and inspirations here....

_____

_____

_____

_____

_____

_____

_____

_____

_____

_____

_____

_____

_____

_____

_____

_____

_____

Notes

Believe in Yourself

Write down your thoughts and inspirations here….

_____

_____

_____

_____

_____

_____

_____

_____

_____

_____

_____

_____

_____

_____

_____

_____

_____

Notes

Imagine Yourself Already Having What You Desire

Write down your thoughts and inspirations here....

_____

_____

_____

_____

_____

_____

_____

_____

_____

_____

_____

_____

_____

_____

_____

_____

_____

_____

Notes

Believe in Yourself

Write down your thoughts and inspirations here....

_____

_____

_____

_____

_____

_____

_____

_____

_____

_____

_____

_____

_____

_____

_____

_____

_____

Notes

Imagine Yourself Already Having What You Desire

Write down your thoughts and inspirations here….

_____

_____

_____

_____

_____

_____

_____

_____

_____

_____

_____

_____

_____

_____

_____

_____

_____

_____

_____

Notes

Believe in Yourself

Write down your thoughts and inspirations here….

Notes

Imagine Yourself Already Having What You Desire

Write down your thoughts and inspirations here....

_____

_____

_____

_____

_____

_____

_____

_____

_____

_____

_____

_____

_____

_____

_____

_____

Notes

Believe in Yourself

Write down your thoughts and inspirations here….

_____

_____

_____

_____

_____

_____

_____

_____

_____

_____

_____

_____

_____

_____

_____

_____

_____

_____

Notes

Imagine Yourself Already Having What You Desire

Write down your thoughts and inspirations here....

_____

_____

_____

_____

_____

_____

_____

_____

_____

_____

_____

_____

_____

_____

_____

_____

_____

_____

Notes

Believe in Yourself

Write down your thoughts and inspirations here….

_____

_____

_____

_____

_____

_____

_____

_____

_____

_____

_____

_____

_____

_____

_____

_____

_____

_____

Notes

Imagine Yourself Already Having What You Desire

Write down your thoughts and inspirations here….

_____

_____

_____

_____

_____

_____

_____

_____

_____

_____

_____

_____

_____

_____

_____

_____

_____

_____

Notes

Believe in Yourself

Write down your thoughts and inspirations here….

_____

_____

_____

_____

_____

_____

_____

_____

_____

_____

_____

_____

_____

_____

_____

_____

_____

_____

_____

Notes

Imagine Yourself Already Having What You Desire

Write down your thoughts and inspirations here....

_____

_____

_____

_____

_____

_____

_____

_____

_____

_____

_____

_____

_____

_____

_____

_____

Notes

Believe in Yourself

Write down your thoughts and inspirations here….

_____

_____

_____

_____

_____

_____

_____

_____

_____

_____

_____

_____

_____

_____

_____

_____

Notes

Imagine Yourself Already Having What You Desire

Write down your thoughts and inspirations here….

_____

_____

_____

_____

_____

_____

_____

_____

_____

_____

_____

_____

_____

_____

_____

_____

_____

Notes

Believe in Yourself

Write down your thoughts and inspirations here....

_____

_____

_____

_____

_____

_____

_____

_____

_____

_____

_____

_____

_____

_____

_____

_____

_____

_____

Notes

Imagine Yourself Already Having What You Desire

Write down your thoughts and inspirations here….

_____

_____

_____

_____

_____

_____

_____

_____

_____

_____

_____

_____

_____

_____

_____

_____

_____

_____

_____

Notes

Believe in Yourself

Write down your thoughts and inspirations here....

_____

_____

_____

_____

_____

_____

_____

_____

_____

_____

_____

_____

_____

_____

_____

_____

_____

_____

Notes

Imagine Yourself Already Having What You Desire

Write down your thoughts and inspirations here….

_____

_____

_____

_____

_____

_____

_____

_____

_____

_____

_____

_____

_____

_____

_____

_____

_____

Notes

Believe in Yourself

Write down your thoughts and inspirations here....

_____

_____

_____

_____

_____

_____

_____

_____

_____

_____

_____

_____

_____

_____

_____

_____

_____

Notes

Imagine Yourself Already Having What You Desire

Write down your thoughts and inspirations here....

_____

_____

_____

_____

_____

_____

_____

_____

_____

_____

_____

_____

_____

_____

_____

_____

Notes

Believe in Yourself

Write down your thoughts and inspirations here....

_____

_____

_____

_____

_____

_____

_____

_____

_____

_____

_____

_____

_____

_____

_____

_____

_____

Notes

Imagine Yourself Already Having What You Desire

Write down your thoughts and inspirations here....

_____

_____

_____

_____

_____

_____

_____

_____

_____

_____

_____

_____

_____

_____

_____

_____

_____

Notes

Believe in Yourself

Write down your thoughts and inspirations here….

_____

_____

_____

_____

_____

_____

_____

_____

_____

_____

_____

_____

_____

_____

_____

_____

_____

_____

Notes

Imagine Yourself Already Having What You Desire

Write down your thoughts and inspirations here….

_____
_____
_____
_____
_____
_____
_____
_____
_____
_____
_____
_____
_____
_____
_____
_____
_____

Notes

Believe in Yourself

Write down your thoughts and inspirations here….

Notes

Imagine Yourself Already Having What You Desire

Write down your thoughts and inspirations here….

_____

_____

_____

_____

_____

_____

_____

_____

_____

_____

_____

_____

_____

_____

_____

_____

_____

_____

_____

_____

_____

Notes

Believe in Yourself

Write down your thoughts and inspirations here….

_____

_____

_____

_____

_____

_____

_____

_____

_____

_____

_____

_____

_____

_____

_____

_____

_____

_____

Notes

Imagine Yourself Already Having What You Desire

Write down your thoughts and inspirations here....

_____

_____

_____

_____

_____

_____

_____

_____

_____

_____

_____

_____

_____

_____

_____

_____

_____

_____

Notes

Believe in Yourself

Write down your thoughts and inspirations here….

_____

_____

_____

_____

_____

_____

_____

_____

_____

_____

_____

_____

_____

_____

_____

_____

_____

_____

Notes

Imagine Yourself Already Having What You Desire

Write down your thoughts and inspirations here….

_____

_____

_____

_____

_____

_____

_____

_____

_____

_____

_____

_____

_____

_____

_____

_____

_____

Notes

Believe in Yourself

Write down your thoughts and inspirations here….

_____

_____

_____

_____

_____

_____

_____

_____

_____

_____

_____

_____

_____

_____

_____

_____

_____

Notes

Imagine Yourself Already Having What You Desire

Write down your thoughts and inspirations here….

_____

_____

_____

_____

_____

_____

_____

_____

_____

_____

_____

_____

_____

_____

_____

_____

_____

Notes

Believe in Yourself

Write down your thoughts and inspirations here....

_____

_____

_____

_____

_____

_____

_____

_____

_____

_____

_____

_____

_____

_____

_____

_____

_____

_____

Notes

Imagine Yourself Already Having What You Desire

Write down your thoughts and inspirations here....

_____

_____

_____

_____

_____

_____

_____

_____

_____

_____

_____

_____

_____

_____

_____

_____

_____

_____

Notes

Believe in Yourself

Write down your thoughts and inspirations here....

_____

_____

_____

_____

_____

_____

_____

_____

_____

_____

_____

_____

_____

_____

_____

_____

_____

Notes

Imagine Yourself Already Having What You Desire

Write down your thoughts and inspirations here....

_____

_____

_____

_____

_____

_____

_____

_____

_____

_____

_____

_____

_____

_____

_____

_____

_____

Notes

Believe in Yourself

Write down your thoughts and inspirations here….

_____

_____

_____

_____

_____

_____

_____

_____

_____

_____

_____

_____

_____

_____

_____

_____

_____

Notes

Imagine Yourself Already Having What You Desire

Write down your thoughts and inspirations here….

_____

_____

_____

_____

_____

_____

_____

_____

_____

_____

_____

_____

_____

_____

_____

_____

_____

Notes

Believe in Yourself

Write down your thoughts and inspirations here….

_____

_____

_____

_____

_____

_____

_____

_____

_____

_____

_____

_____

_____

_____

_____

_____

_____

_____

Notes

Imagine Yourself Already Having What You Desire

Write down your thoughts and inspirations here….

_____

_____

_____

_____

_____

_____

_____

_____

_____

_____

_____

_____

_____

_____

_____

_____

_____

_____

_____

_____

Notes

Believe in Yourself

Write down your thoughts and inspirations here....

_____

_____

_____

_____

_____

_____

_____

_____

_____

_____

_____

_____

_____

_____

_____

_____

_____

_____

_____

_____

Notes

Imagine Yourself Already Having What You Desire

Write down your thoughts and inspirations here….

_____

_____

_____

_____

_____

_____

_____

_____

_____

_____

_____

_____

_____

_____

_____

_____

Notes

Believe in Yourself

Write down your thoughts and inspirations here….

_____

_____

_____

_____

_____

_____

_____

_____

_____

_____

_____

_____

_____

_____

_____

_____

Notes

Imagine Yourself Already Having What You Desire

Write down your thoughts and inspirations here….

_____

_____

_____

_____

_____

_____

_____

_____

_____

_____

_____

_____

_____

_____

_____

_____

_____

_____

Notes

Believe in Yourself

Write down your thoughts and inspirations here….

_____

_____

_____

_____

_____

_____

_____

_____

_____

_____

_____

_____

_____

_____

_____

_____

_____

_____

Notes

Imagine Yourself Already Having What You Desire

Write down your thoughts and inspirations here….

_____

_____

_____

_____

_____

_____

_____

_____

_____

_____

_____

_____

_____

_____

_____

_____

_____

Notes

Believe in Yourself

Write down your thoughts and inspirations here….

_____

_____

_____

_____

_____

_____

_____

_____

_____

_____

_____

_____

_____

_____

_____

_____

_____

_____

Notes

Imagine Yourself Already Having What You Desire

Write down your thoughts and inspirations here….

_____

_____

_____

_____

_____

_____

_____

_____

_____

_____

_____

_____

_____

_____

_____

_____

_____

_____

Notes

Believe in Yourself

Write down your thoughts and inspirations here....

_____

_____

_____

_____

_____

_____

_____

_____

_____

_____

_____

_____

_____

_____

_____

_____

_____

Notes

Imagine Yourself Already Having What You Desire

Write down your thoughts and inspirations here....

Notes

Believe in Yourself

Write down your thoughts and inspirations here....

_____

_____

_____

_____

_____

_____

_____

_____

_____

_____

_____

_____

_____

_____

_____

_____

_____

_____

Notes

Imagine Yourself Already Having What You Desire

Write down your thoughts and inspirations here....

_____

_____

_____

_____

_____

_____

_____

_____

_____

_____

_____

_____

_____

_____

_____

_____

_____

Notes

Believe in Yourself

Write down your thoughts and inspirations here....

_____

_____

_____

_____

_____

_____

_____

_____

_____

_____

_____

_____

_____

_____

_____

_____

_____

Notes

Imagine Yourself Already Having What You Desire

Write down your thoughts and inspirations here....

_____

_____

_____

_____

_____

_____

_____

_____

_____

_____

_____

_____

_____

_____

_____

_____

Notes

Believe in Yourself

Write down your thoughts and inspirations here….

_____

_____

_____

_____

_____

_____

_____

_____

_____

_____

_____

_____

_____

_____

_____

_____

_____

Notes

Imagine Yourself Already Having What You Desire

Write down your thoughts and inspirations here....

_____

_____

_____

_____

_____

_____

_____

_____

_____

_____

_____

_____

_____

_____

_____

_____

_____

_____

Notes

Believe in Yourself

Write down your thoughts and inspirations here….

_____

_____

_____

_____

_____

_____

_____

_____

_____

_____

_____

_____

_____

_____

_____

_____

_____

Notes

Imagine Yourself Already Having What You Desire

Write down your thoughts and inspirations here….

_____

_____

_____

_____

_____

_____

_____

_____

_____

_____

_____

_____

_____

_____

_____

_____

_____

_____

Notes

Believe in Yourself

Write down your thoughts and inspirations here….

_____

_____

_____

_____

_____

_____

_____

_____

_____

_____

_____

_____

_____

_____

_____

_____

_____

Notes

Imagine Yourself Already Having What You Desire

Write down your thoughts and inspirations here....

_____

_____

_____

_____

_____

_____

_____

_____

_____

_____

_____

_____

_____

_____

_____

_____

_____

_____

Notes

Believe in Yourself

Write down your thoughts and inspirations here….

_____

_____

_____

_____

_____

_____

_____

_____

_____

_____

_____

_____

_____

_____

_____

_____

_____

Notes

Imagine Yourself Already Having What You Desire

Write down your thoughts and inspirations here....

_____

_____

_____

_____

_____

_____

_____

_____

_____

_____

_____

_____

_____

_____

_____

_____

_____

Notes

Believe in Yourself

Write down your thoughts and inspirations here….

_____

_____

_____

_____

_____

_____

_____

_____

_____

_____

_____

_____

_____

_____

_____

_____

_____

Notes

Imagine Yourself Already Having What You Desire

Write down your thoughts and inspirations here….

_____

_____

_____

_____

_____

_____

_____

_____

_____

_____

_____

_____

_____

_____

_____

_____

_____

_____

Notes

Believe in Yourself

Write down your thoughts and inspirations here....

_____

_____

_____

_____

_____

_____

_____

_____

_____

_____

_____

_____

_____

_____

_____

_____

_____

_____

Notes

Imagine Yourself Already Having What You Desire

Write down your thoughts and inspirations here....

_____

_____

_____

_____

_____

_____

_____

_____

_____

_____

_____

_____

_____

_____

_____

_____

_____

Notes

Believe in Yourself

Write down your thoughts and inspirations here….

_____

_____

_____

_____

_____

_____

_____

_____

_____

_____

_____

_____

_____

_____

_____

_____

_____

_____

_____

_____

Notes

Imagine Yourself Already Having What You Desire

Write down your thoughts and inspirations here….

_____

_____

_____

_____

_____

_____

_____

_____

_____

_____

_____

_____

_____

_____

_____

_____

_____

_____

Notes

Believe in Yourself

Write down your thoughts and inspirations here....

_____

_____

_____

_____

_____

_____

_____

_____

_____

_____

_____

_____

_____

_____

_____

_____

_____

_____

www.ingramcontent.com/pod-product-compliance
Lightning Source LLC
Chambersburg PA
CBHW020922180526
45163CB00007B/2838